I HATE EX-BOYFRIENDS
COLORING BOOK

Join our mailing list to be among

the first to find out about special offers,

discounts and our new releases!

Sign up at:
www.adultcoloringworld.net

Copyright © 2017 Adult Coloring World
All rights reserved.
ISBN-13: 978-1544686424
ISBN-10: 1544686420

@adultcoloringworld

facebook.com/adultcoloringworldbooks

@adultcolorworld

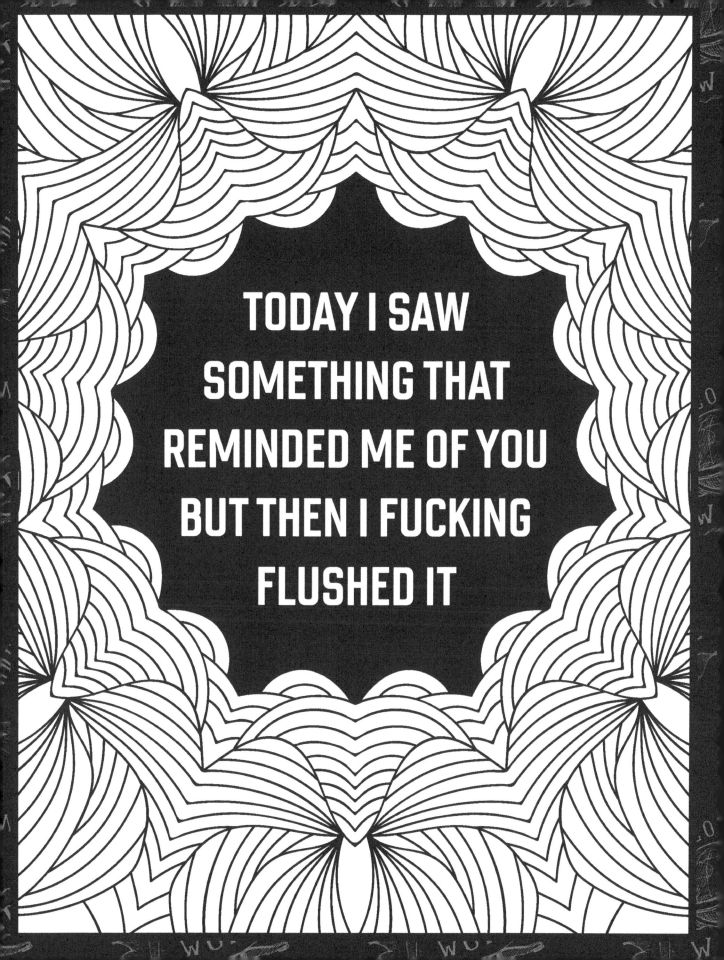

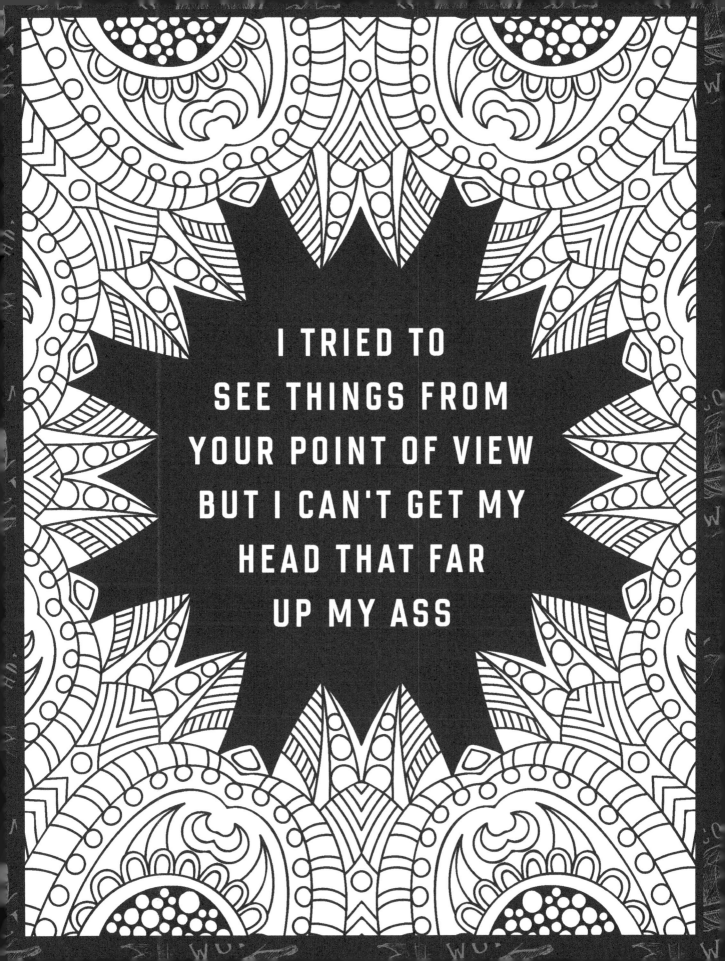

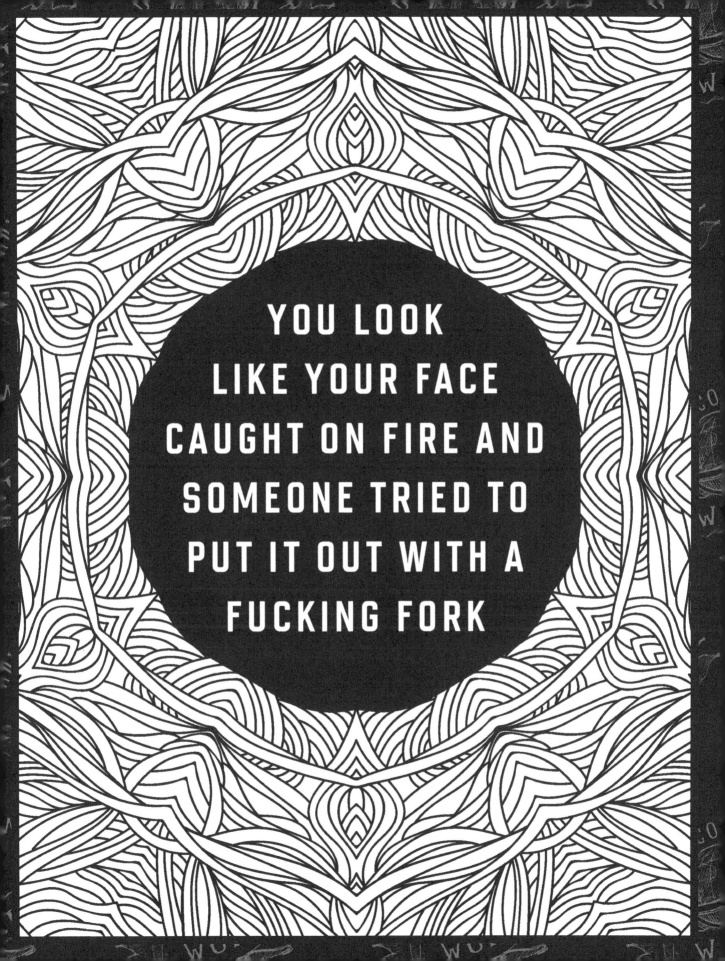

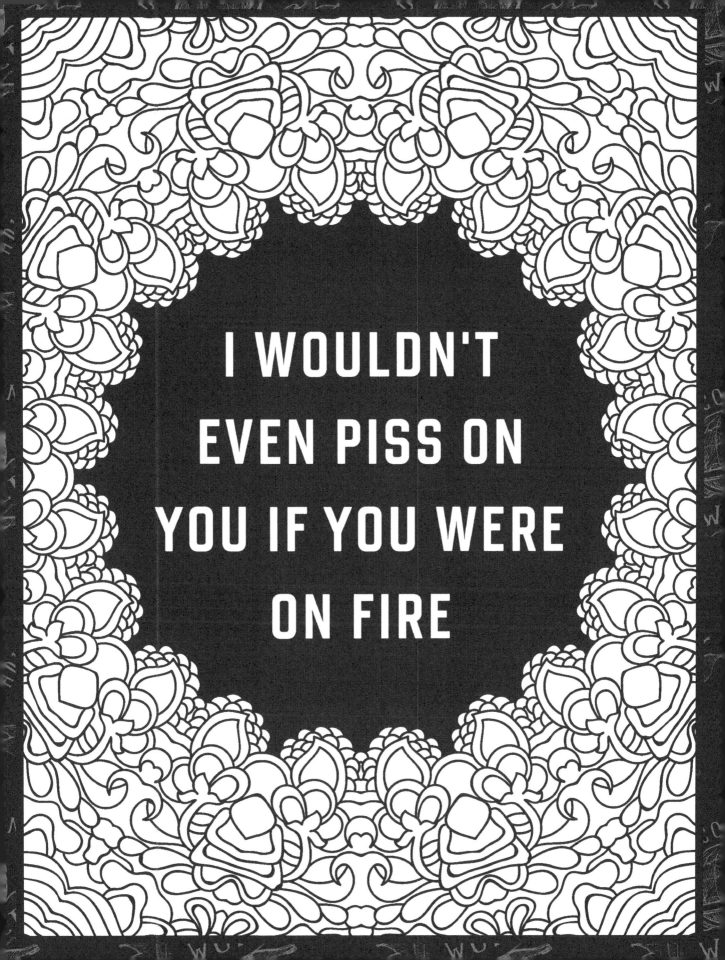

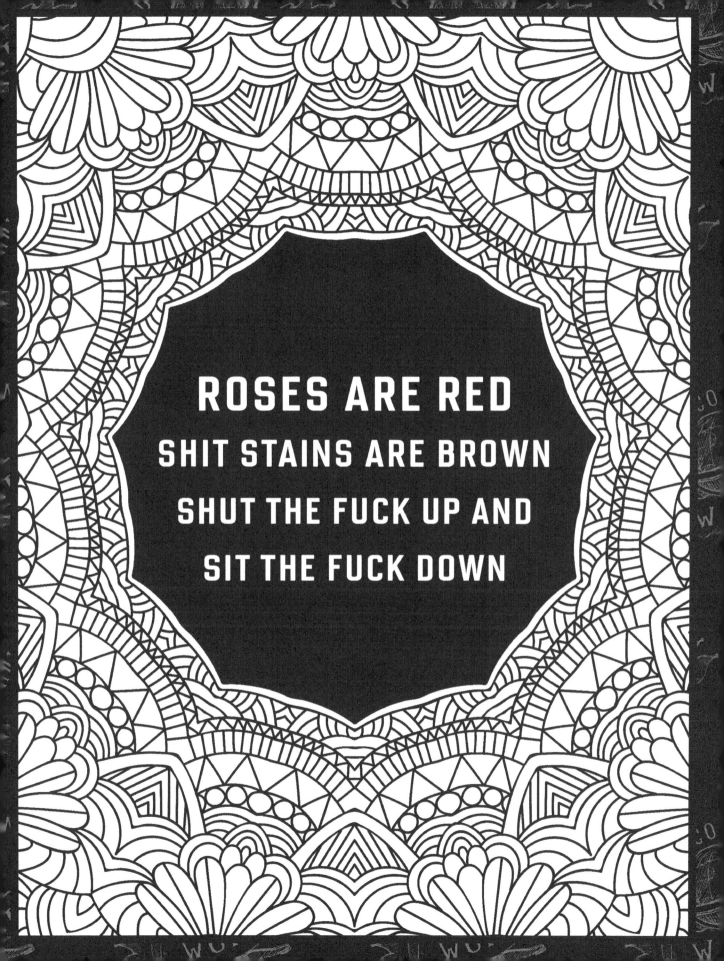

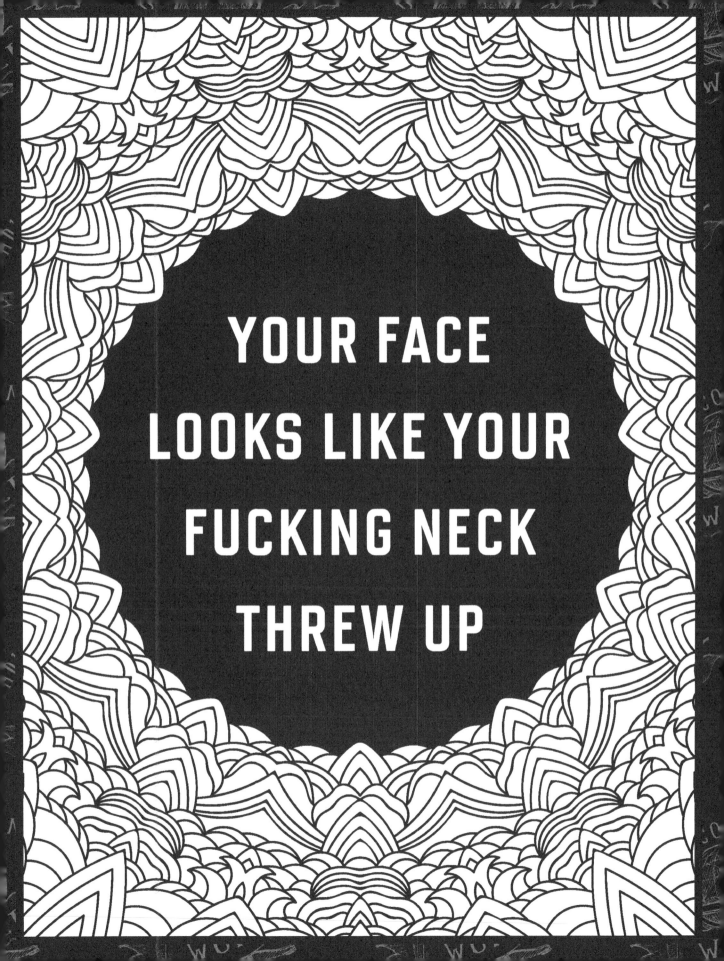

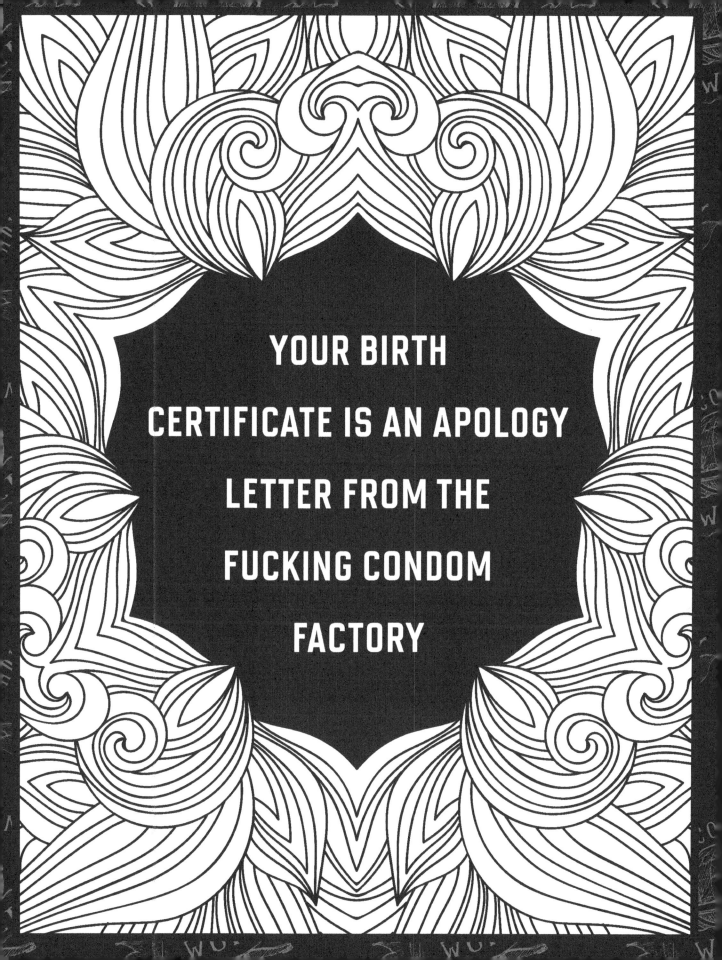

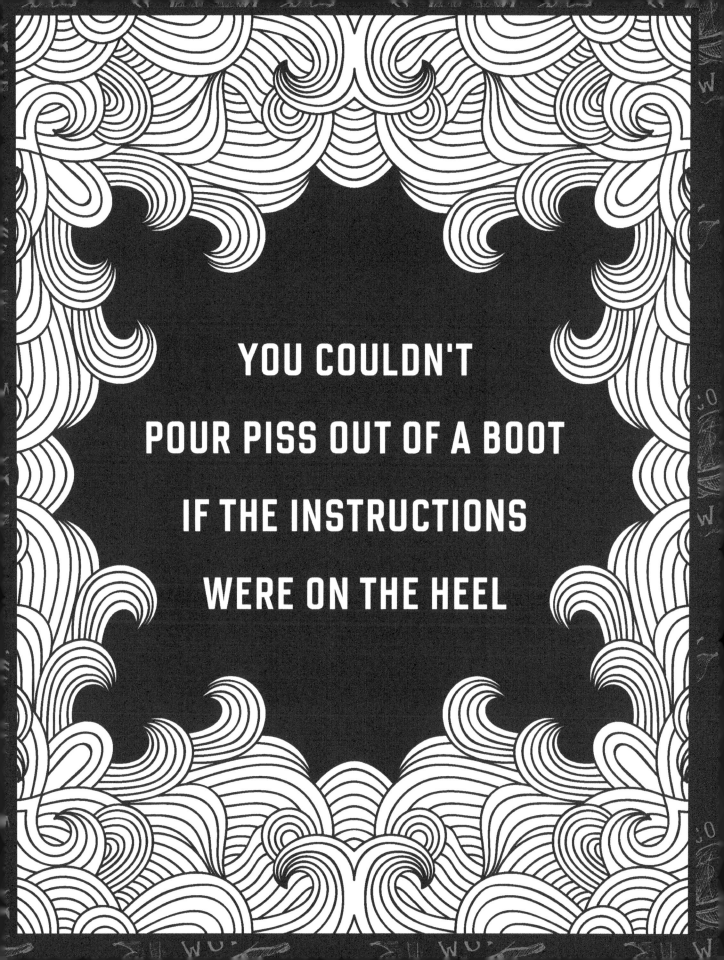

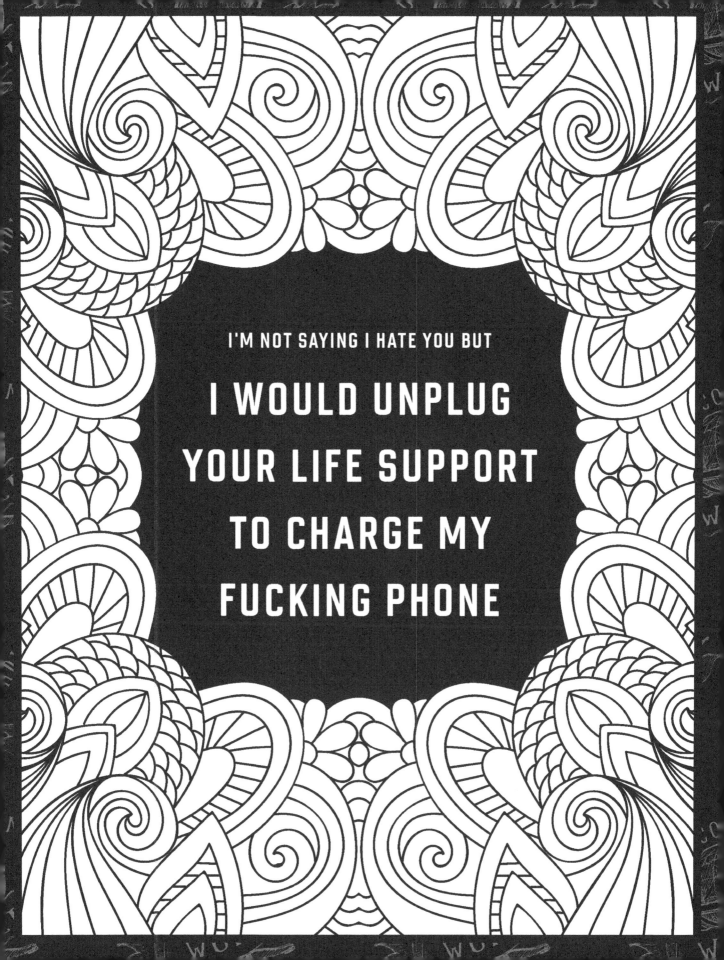

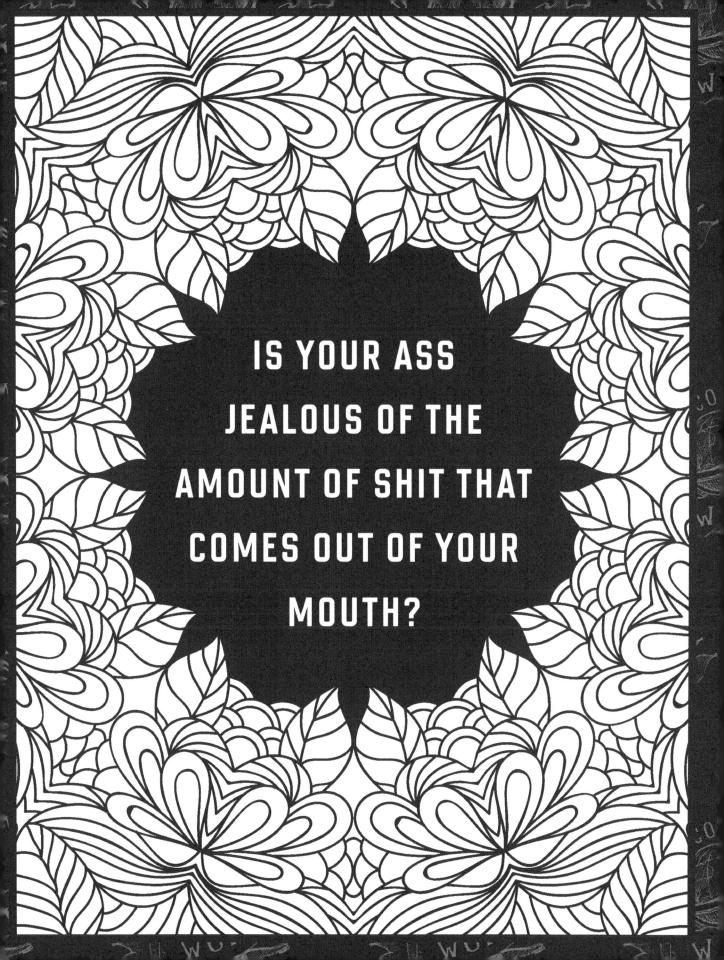

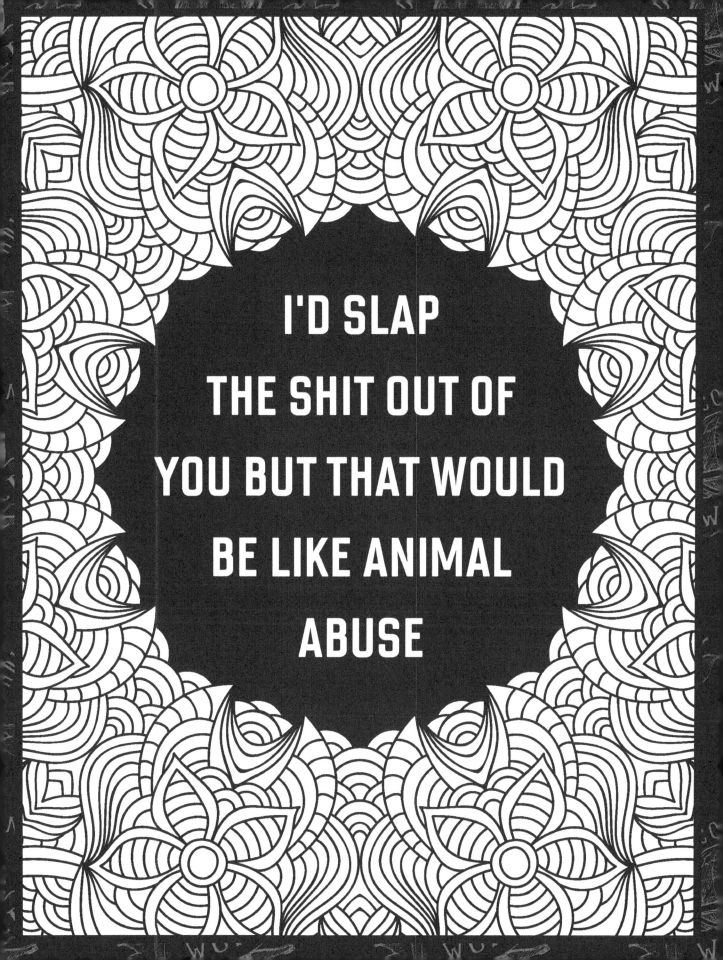

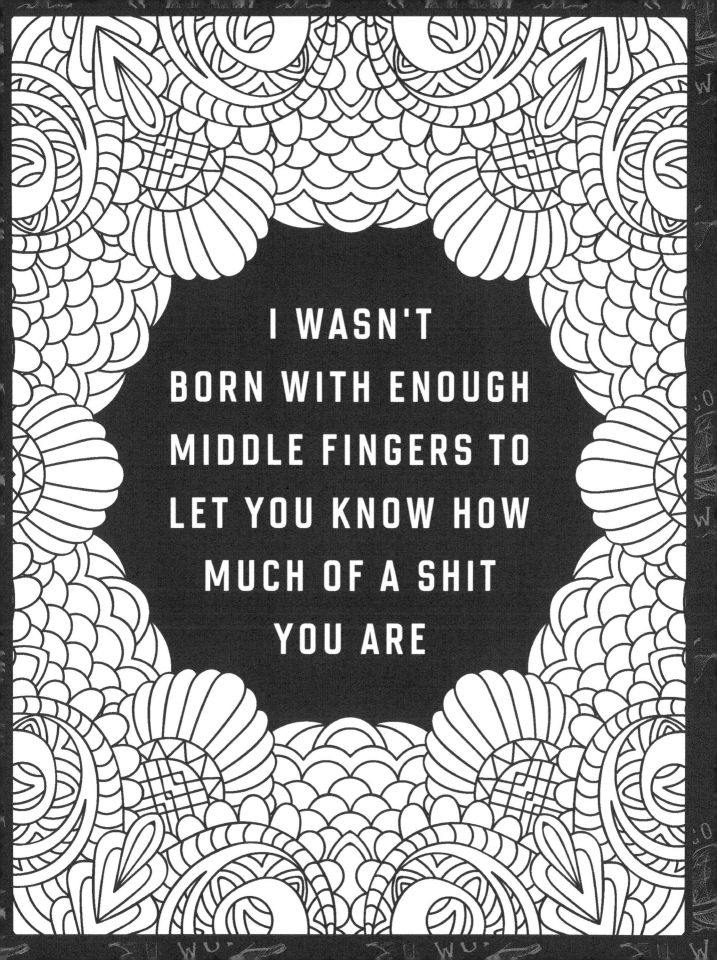

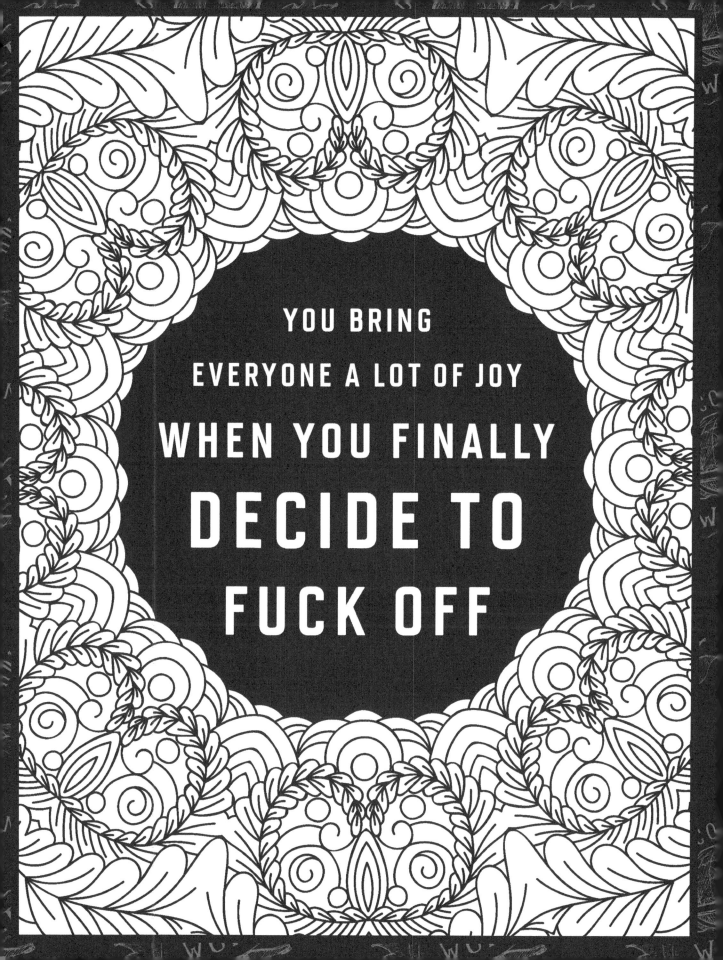

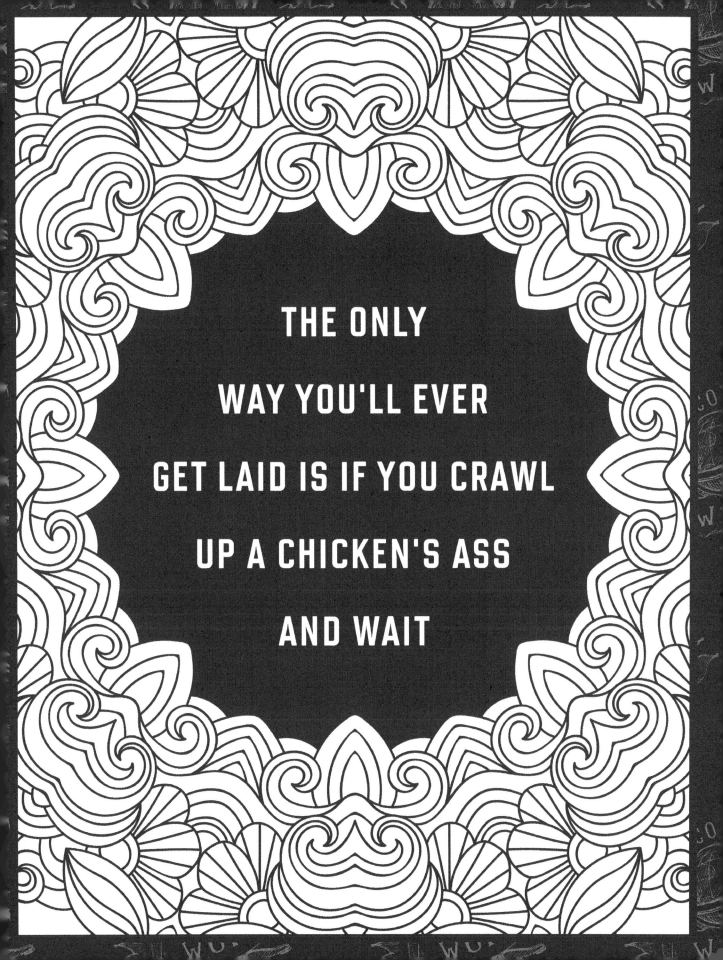

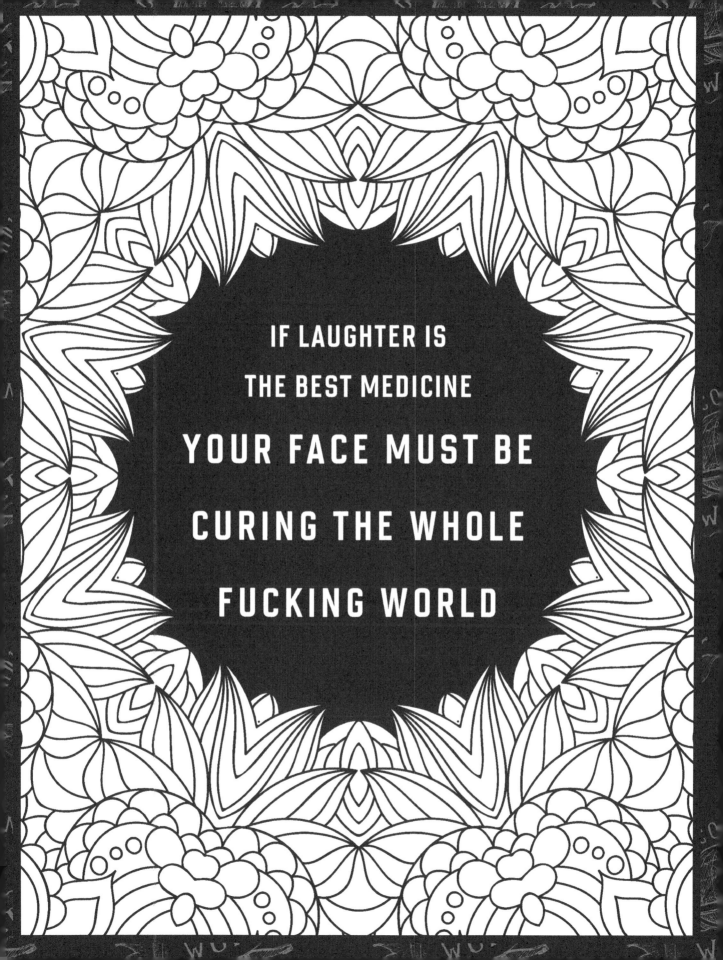

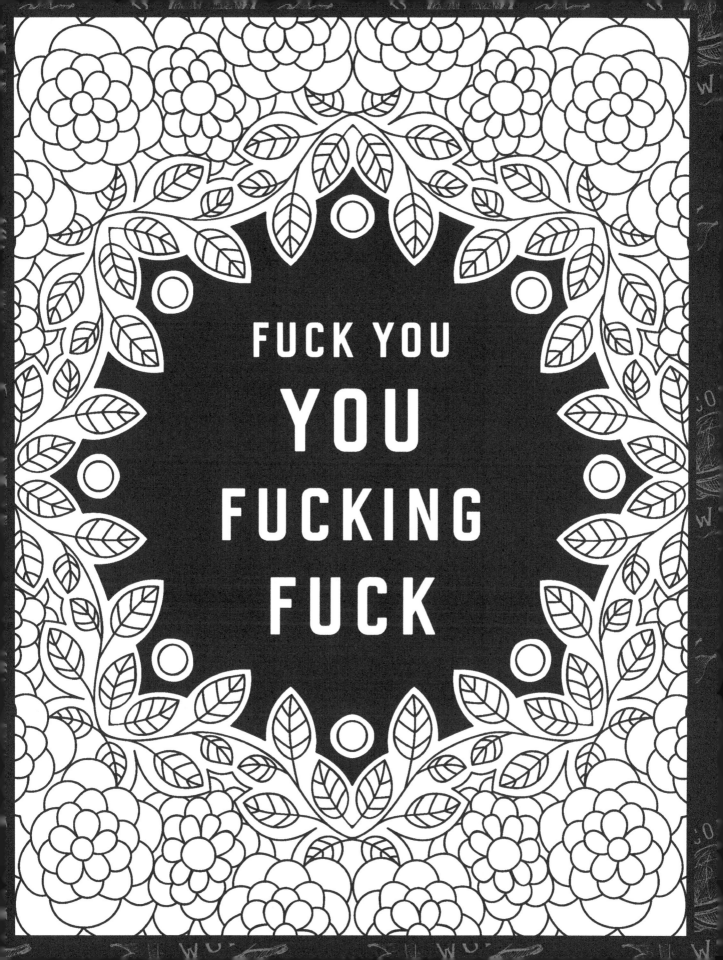

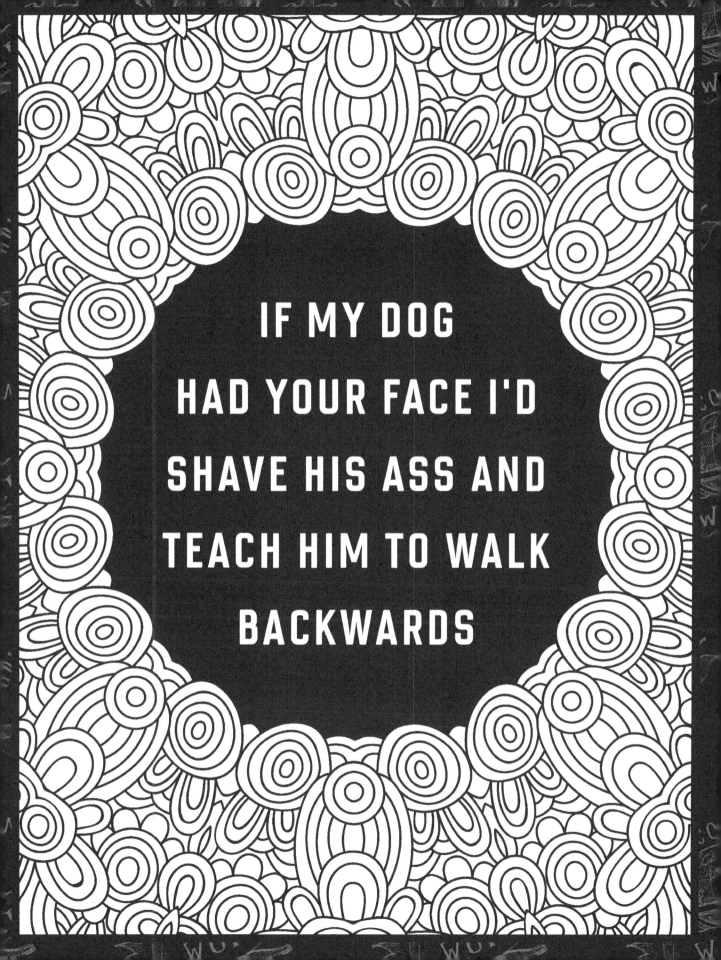

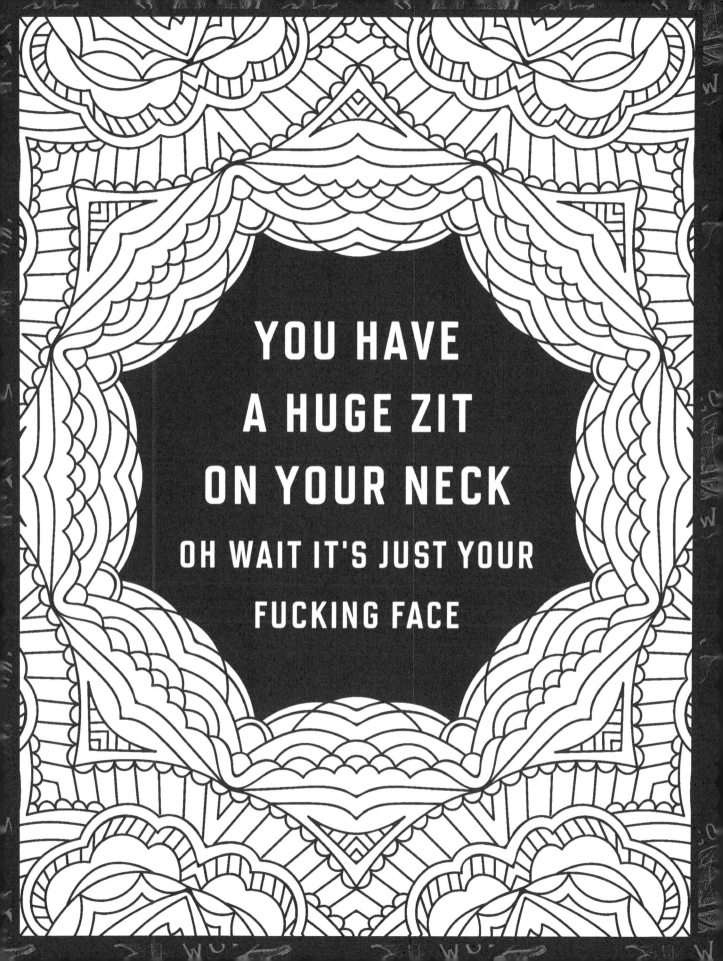

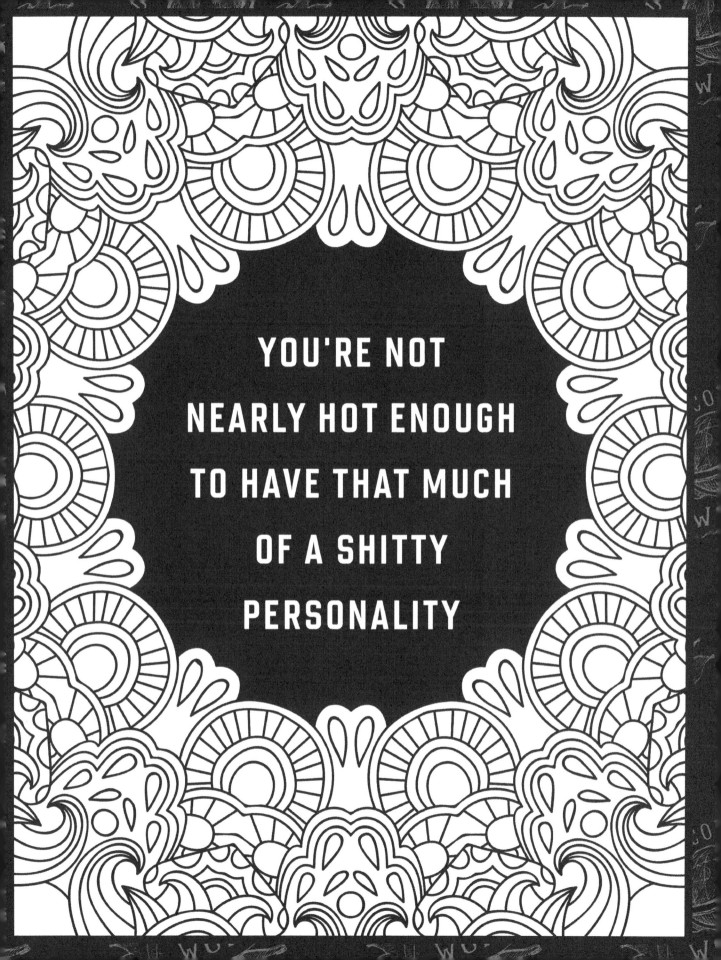

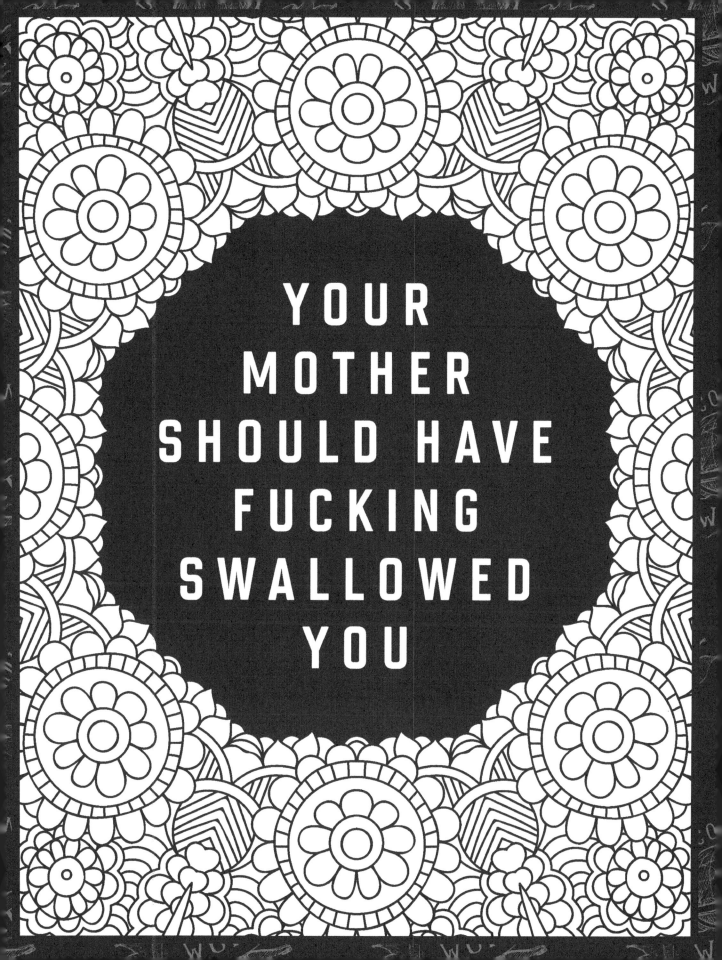

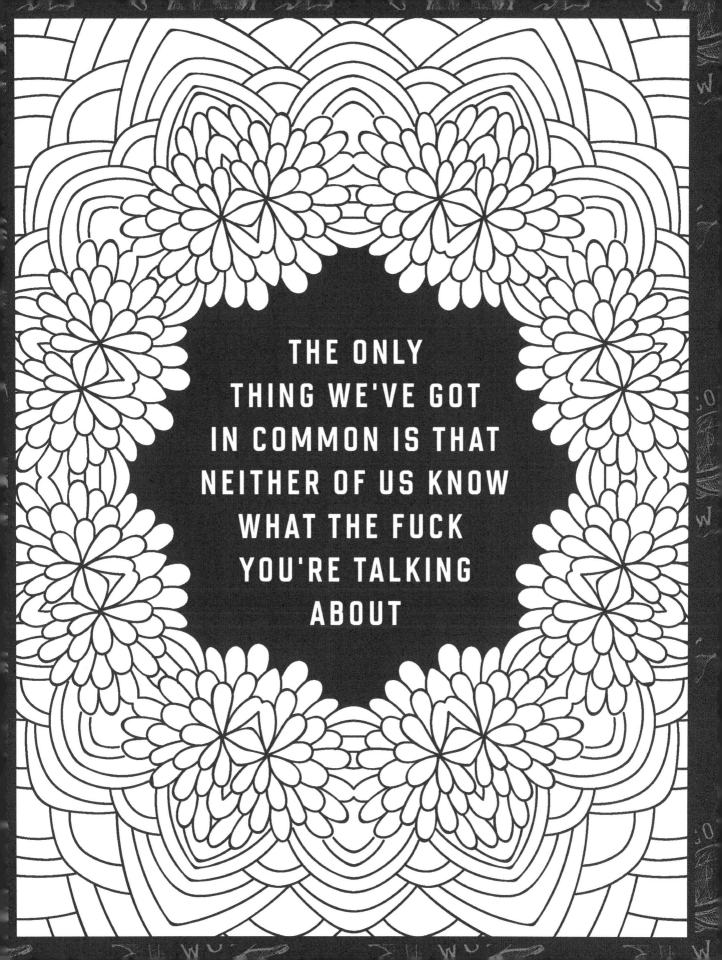

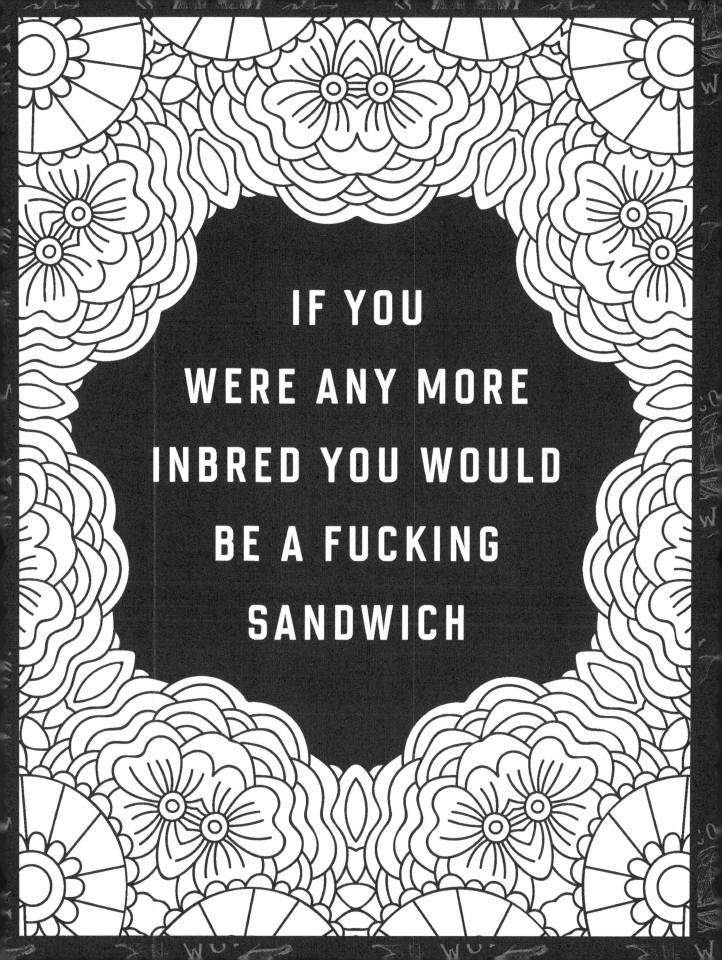

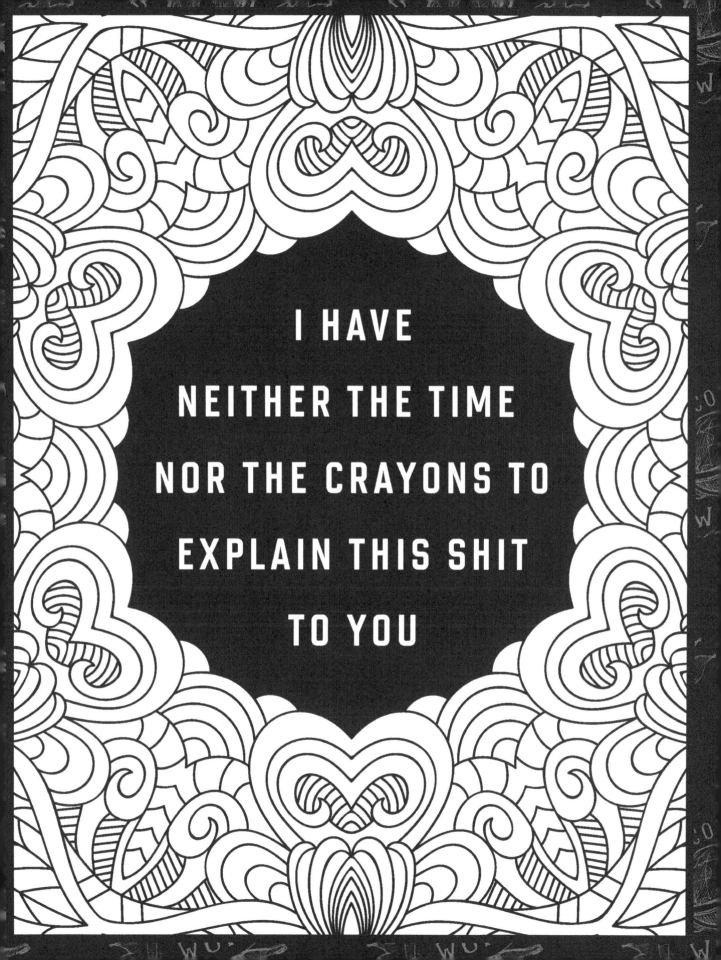

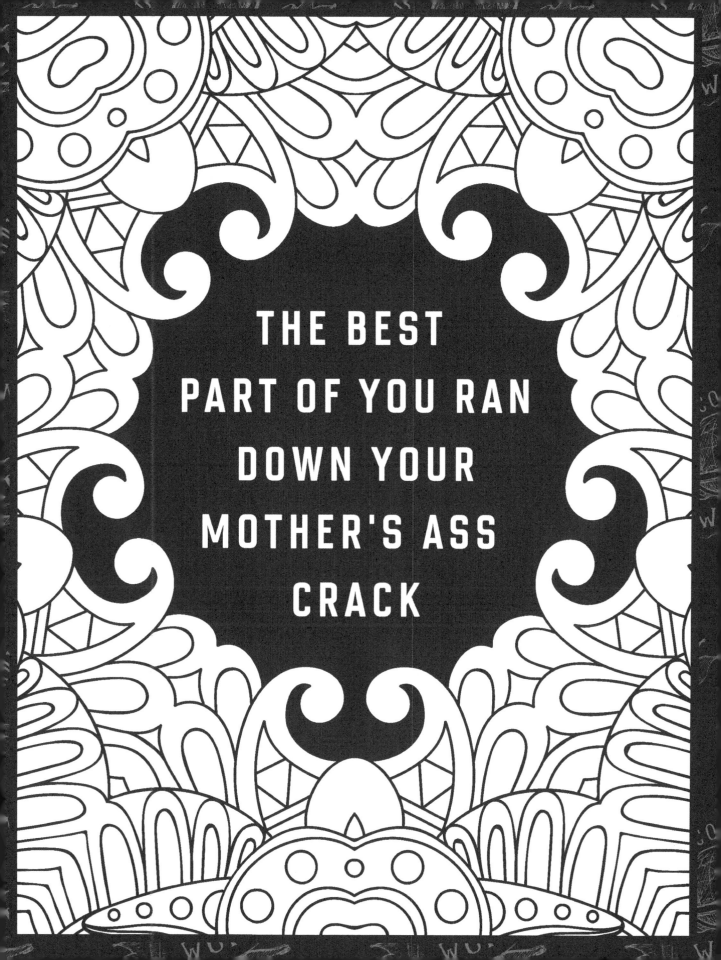

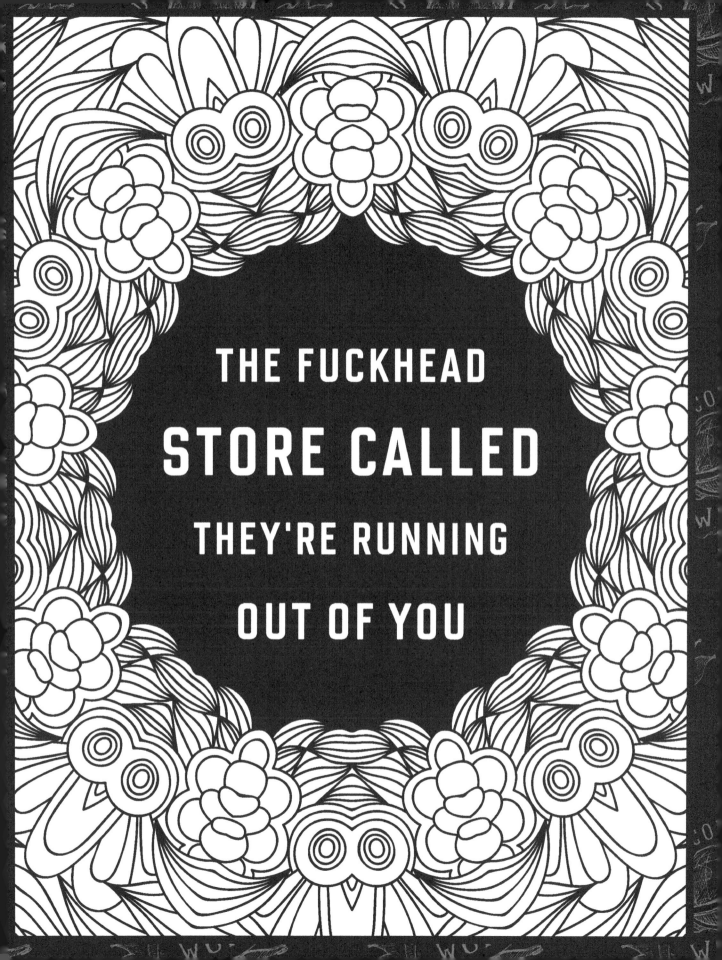

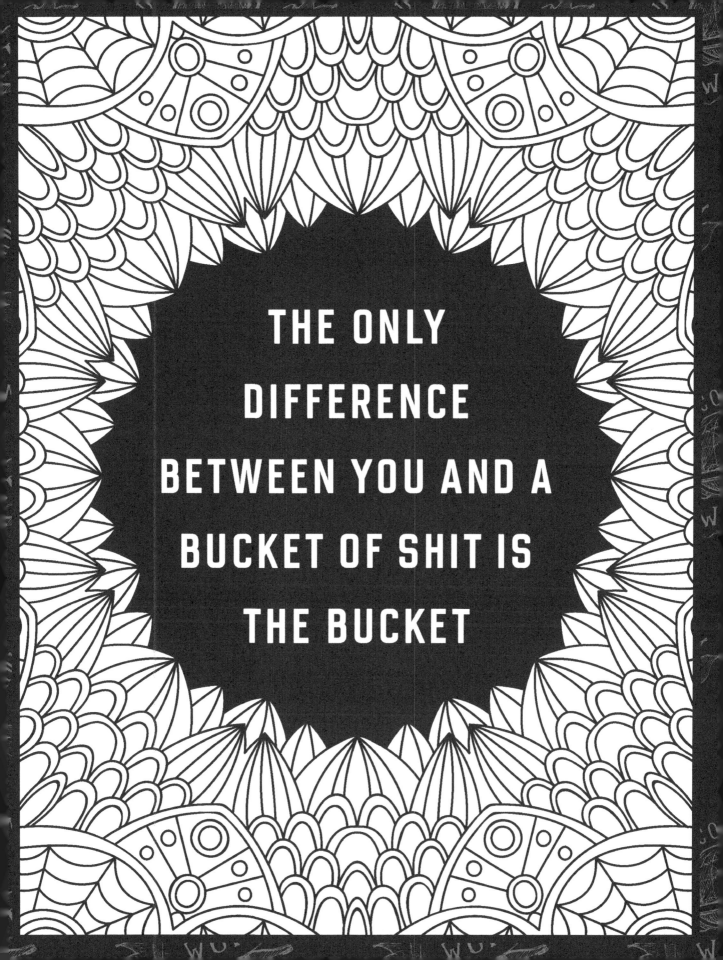

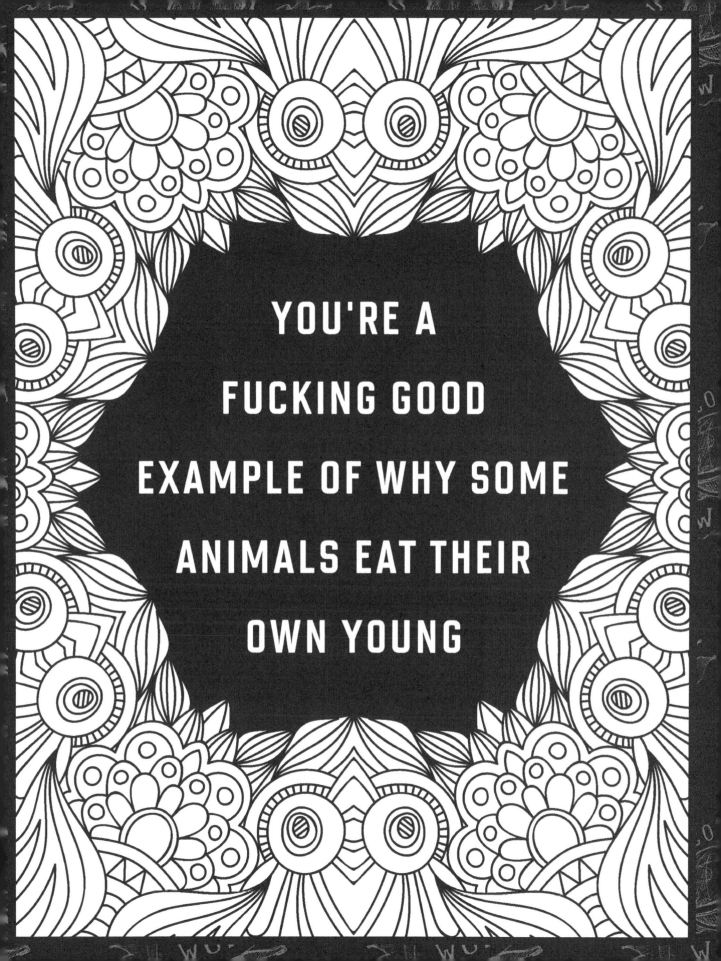

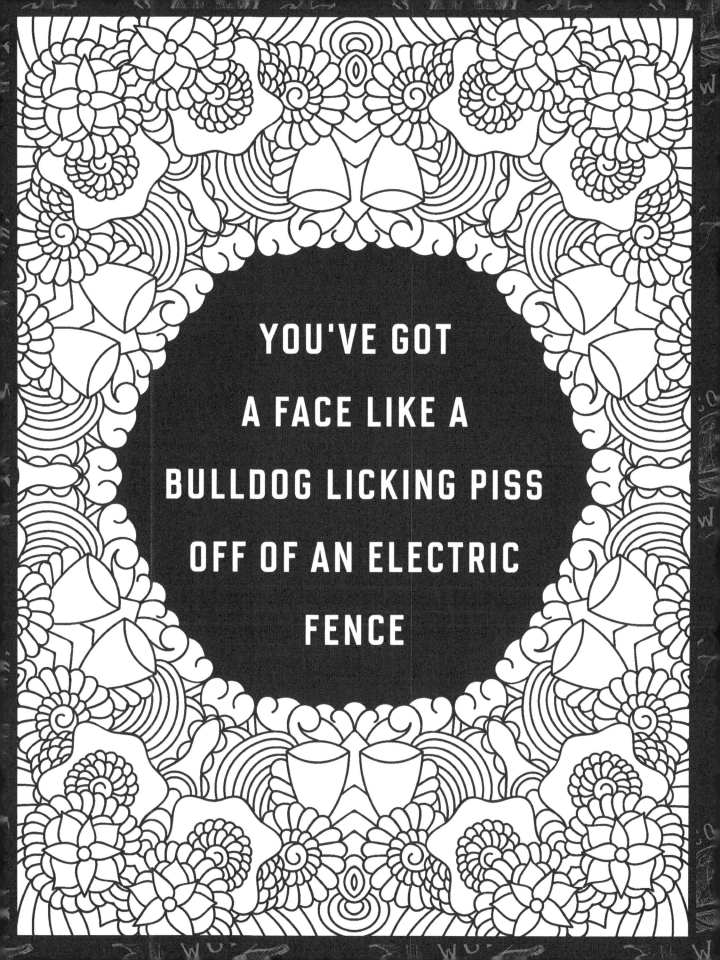

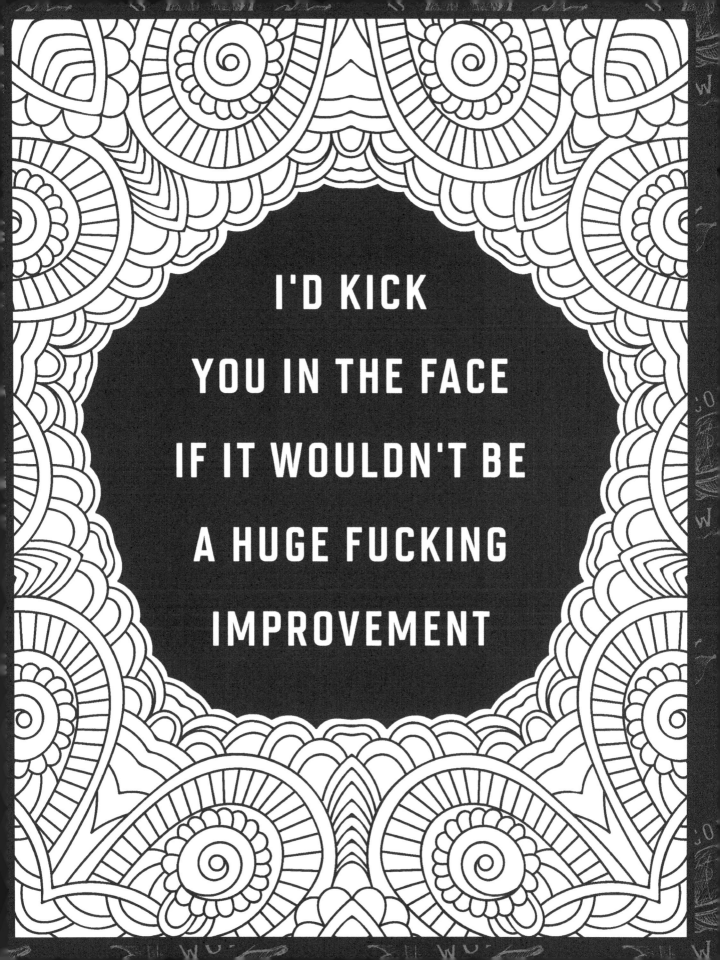

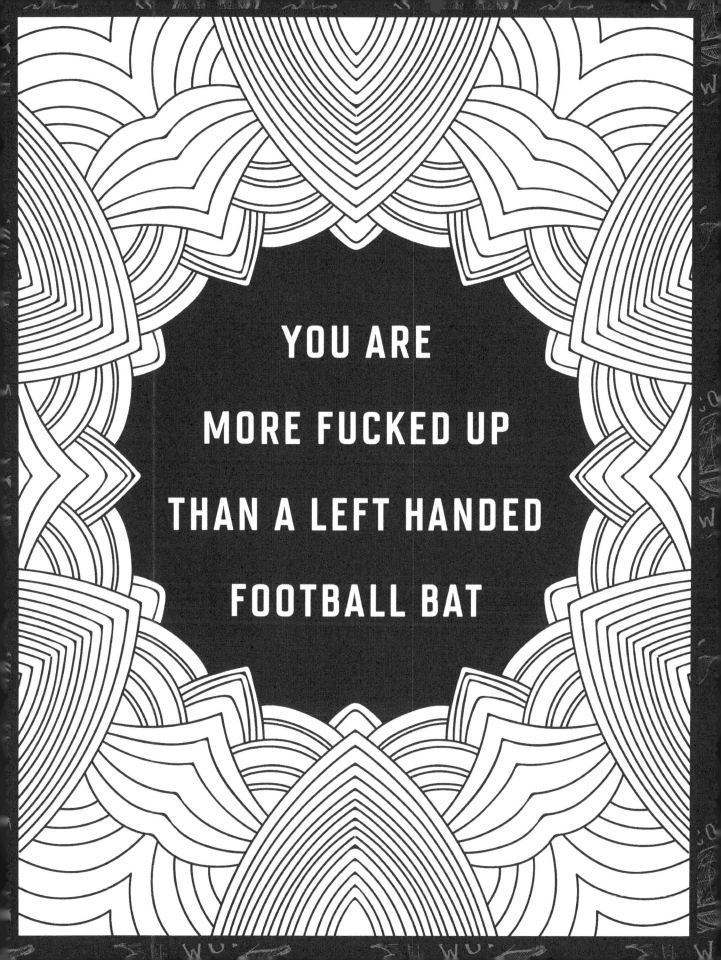

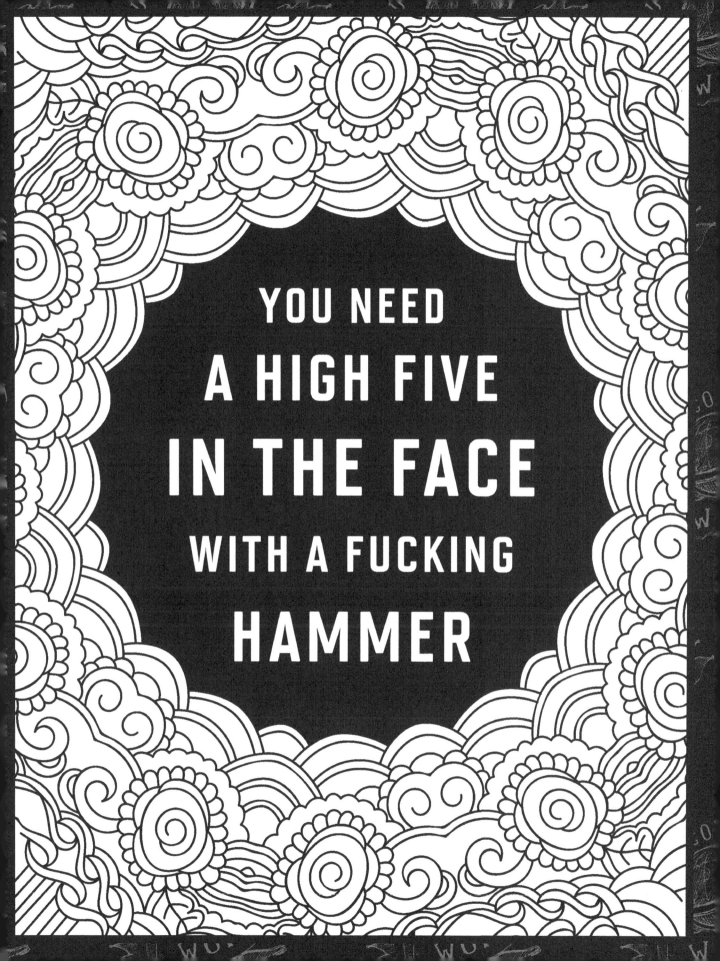

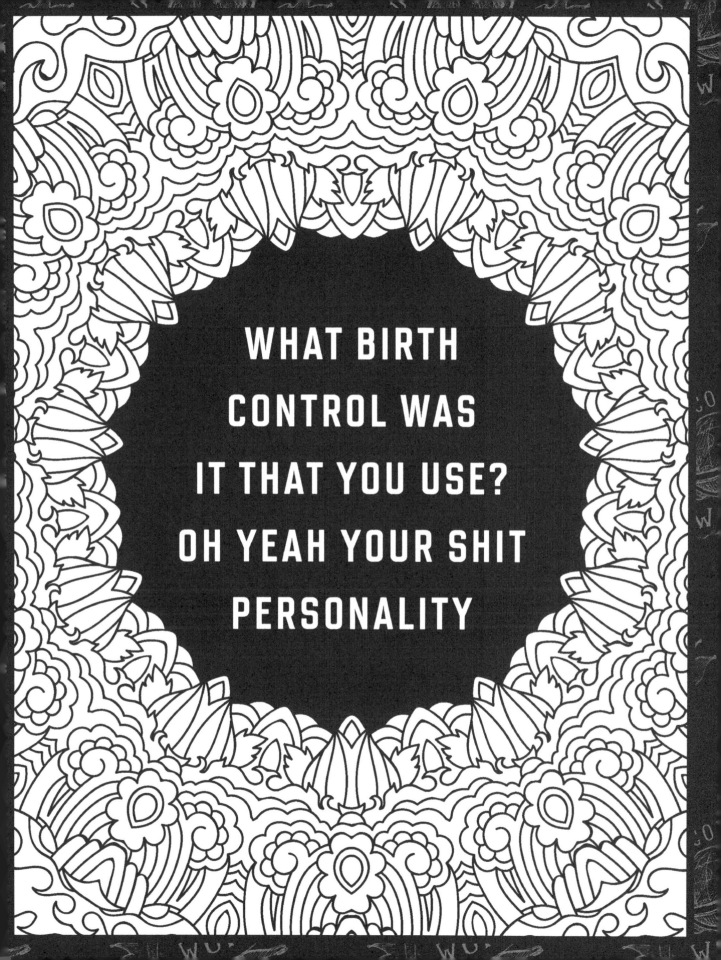

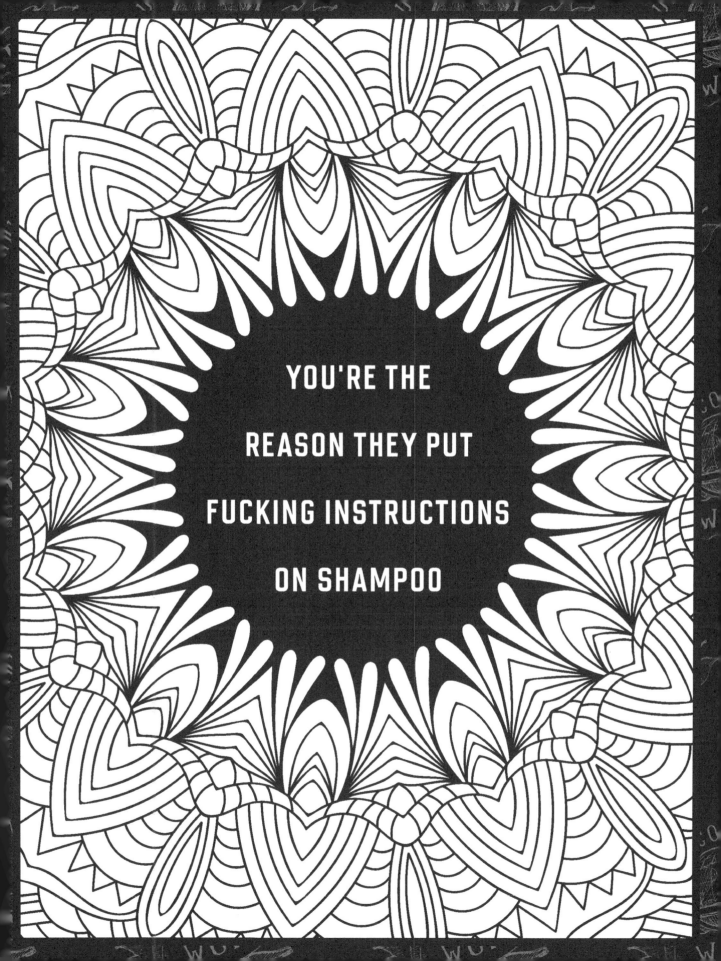

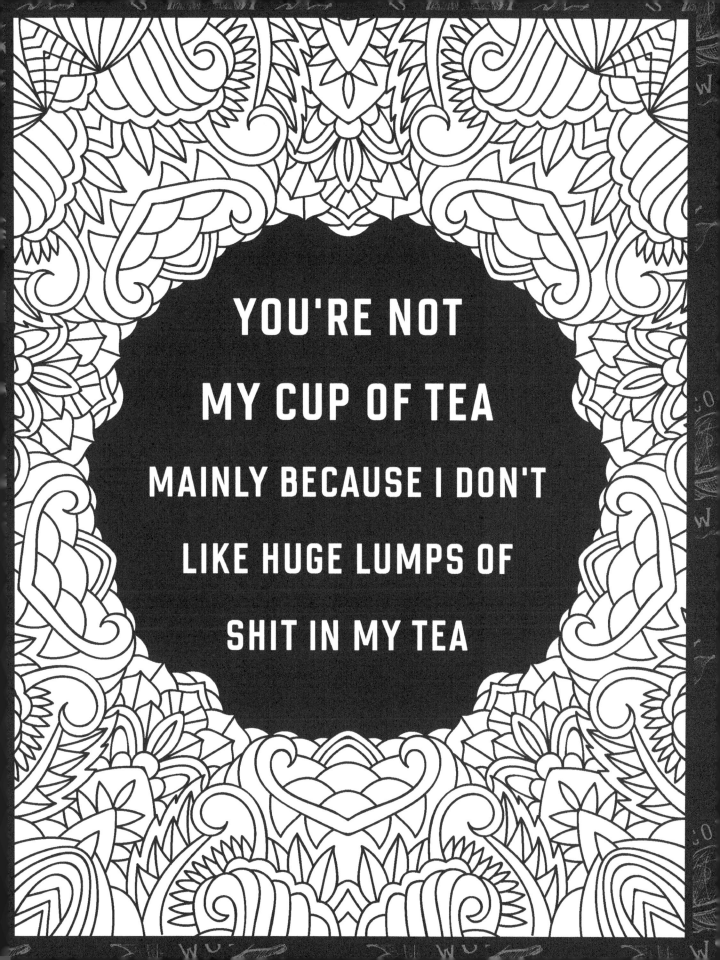

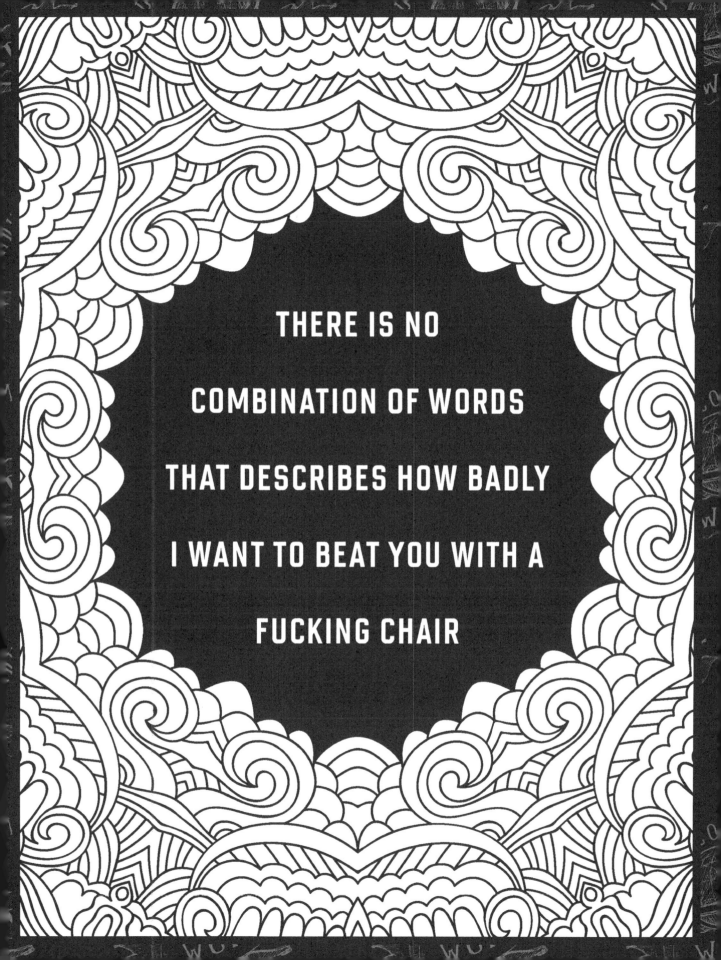

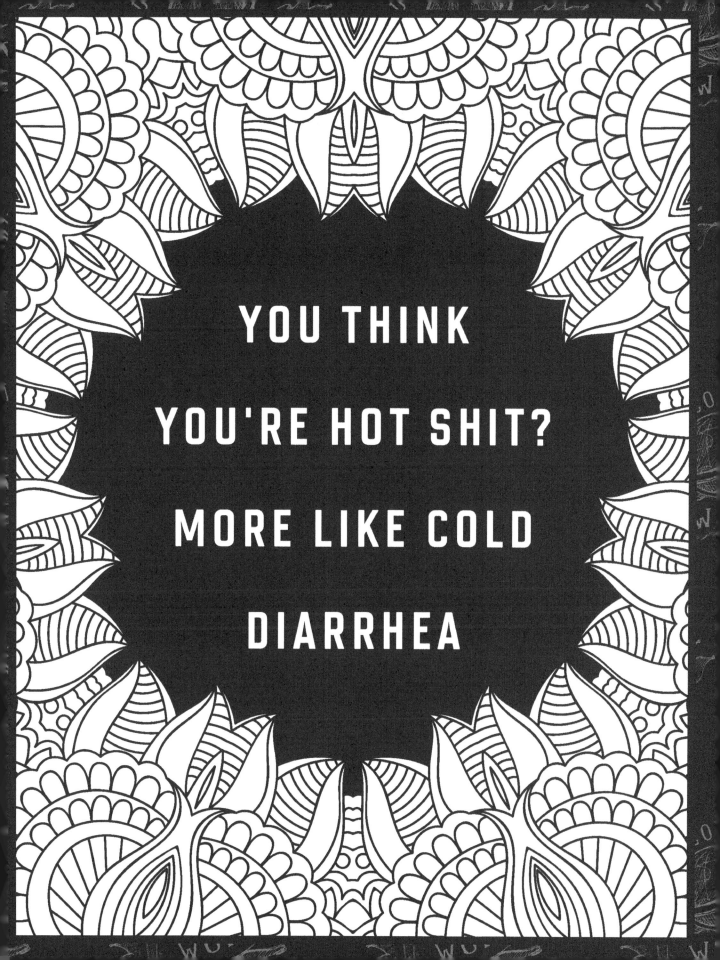

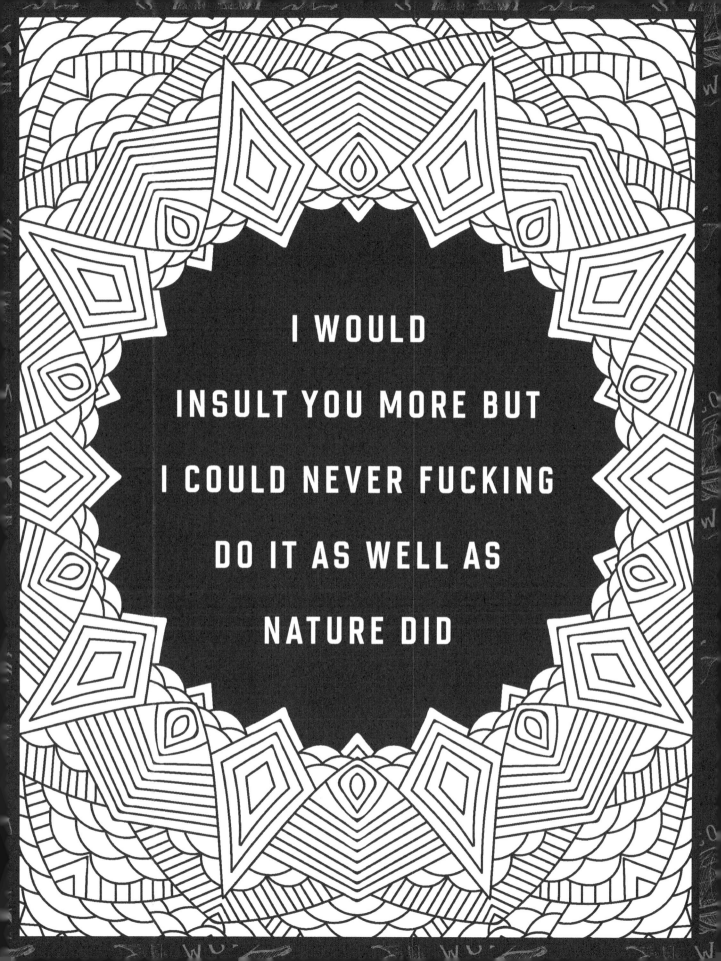

COLOR TEST
PAGE

COLOR TEST PAGE

COLOR TEST PAGE

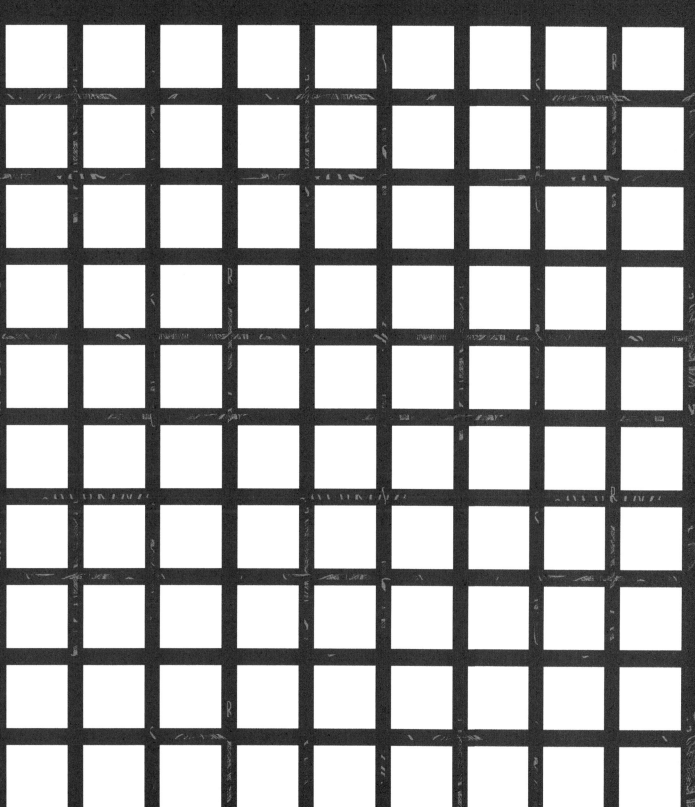

WE HOPE YOU ENJOYED THIS BOOK!

TO VIEW OUR HUGE RANGE OF ADULT COLORING BOOKS, VISIT OUR WEBSITE TODAY AND DON'T FORGET TO FOLLOW US VIA OUR SOCIAL ACCOUNTS!

ADULTCOLORINGWORLD.NET

 @adultcoloringworld

 facebook.com/adultcoloringworldbooks

 @adultcolorworld

Made in United States
Orlando, FL
16 November 2022